"The Rose-Fosse collision is one of the five most memorable moments in All-Star history. And I don't mean in Cincinnati All-Star history. We are talking about all-time, all-everywhere, All-Star memories. And for that matter, a signature moment in Reds history as well. *'HEARD but not SEEN'* looks at it from a surprising, new perspective. It is a definite addition to my baseball bookshelf."

REDS HISTORIAN GREG RHODES

Also by Denny Dressman

[NONFICTION]

Gerry Faust: Notre Dame's Man In Motion

Yes I Can! Yes You Can!

The Diabetes Antidote

Eddie Robinson:
'. . . he was the Martin Luther King of football'

Sterling Heroes of World War II

HEARD
but not SEEN

Richard Nixon, Frank Robinson
and The All-Star Game's
most debated play

By Denny Dressman
(45 years later)

COMSERV BOOKS
L L C

DENVER

For information, contact
ComServ Books
P.O. Box 3116
Greenwood Village, CO 80155-3116
www.comservbooks.com

LCCN 2015906715
ISBN 978-0-9774283-9-7

Printed in the U.S.A.

The cover art is an original illustration by artist Charles Pyle. A native Californian, Pyle attended the Academy of Art College in San Francisco, where he now is Chair of the School of Illustration and teaches the next generation of illustrators. His work has appeared on many book covers and gallery walls, and in magazines and advertising campaigns, and is in many private and government collections. He lives in the California Wine Country with his wife Trina.

For more about Charles Pyle and his art, go to www.charlespylestudio.com

For dad,
who died nine years after
the 1970 All-Star Game.

He taught me how to play the game,
and how to appreciate
its fine points and its rich history
throughout life.

CONTENTS

Down Under

RIVERFRONT STADIUM was aglow. Literally.

Only the fifth *night* All-Star Game in Major League Baseball history had reached the bottom of the sixth inning, and in the midsummer evening sky the lights ringing the upper deck were producing a halo effect above the brand new ballpark alongside the Ohio River. Richard M. Nixon, the 37th President of the United States and an ardent baseball fan, settled into his front row seat.

The American League had moved ahead 1-0 in the top of the sixth on Carl Yastrzemski's jam-job single to center that drove in – as irony that night would have it – Cleveland's Ray Fosse. The Americans' catcher had opened the inning with a single to, yes, Pete Rose in right on the first pitch he saw. If the AL stars could hold that lead, they'd end a seven-year losing streak.

Sam McDowell, the Cleveland lefthander they called Sudden Sam, was in his third inning on the mound for the AL. He walked Dick Allen and Pete Rose to start the bottom of the sixth, but retired Rose's Cincinnati teammate, Tony Perez, and Chicago's Jim Hickman on pop flies to second baseman Davey Johnson of the Orioles. That brought another of Rose's teammates, Johnny Bench, to the plate.

The 51,838 partisan fans anticipated something dramatic from their superstar catcher, who was in the midst of a season that would see him win his first of two National League Most Valuable Player Awards.

But that's not what they got. Sudden Sam, who was leading the major leagues with 183 strikeouts in 173 innings, struck Bench out for the second time in three innings. It was on to the seventh.

As Mr. Nixon recorded a K in the scorecard he was keeping, up in the Press Box came an announcement:

"The stadium elevator will be shut down after the top of the seventh inning by Secret Service until the President leaves the stadium.

"Anyone covering either team's locker room should take the elevator from the press box to the locker room level BEFORE the middle of the seventh. After the top of the seventh, you won't be able to go to the locker rooms until the President has left the stadium.

"You will be able to see the rest of the game on television monitors in the interview room under the stadium."

I was among dozens of reporters who hustled to the Press Box elevator. I was a 25-year-old sports writer, hired at *The Cincinnati Enquirer* by sports editor Jim Schottelkotte less than a year earlier. It was my first All-Star Game.

I had grown up across the river in Northern Kentucky and knew Reds history well, both from firsthand experience and the stories of earlier years my dad told me, at my urging. It was pretty exciting to witness the next chapter in that history as it unfolded.

Little did I – or any of the other writers who went "down under" as the seventh inning began – know what would happen in the game, or to us, in the next two hours.

"Last Pitch" by W. F. Schildman, used with permission of CEI Sports Inc.

Crosley Field

THE 41ST Midsummer Classic was the third
Major League Baseball All-Star Game played in Cincinnati. The first two were held at Crosley Field, the fore-
runner to Riverfront Stadium, in 1938 and 1953.
Those games were historic, too, though not in the controversial way the 1970 game was destined to be.

Known as Redland Field until new Reds owner Powell Crosley Jr. renamed it in 1934, the ballpark at Findlay Street and Western Avenue opened in 1912. Seven years later it was one of the sites of the only "fixed" World Series. That Series was best-of-nine, and the underdog Reds – unaware that eight members of what became known as the "Black Sox" had agreed to throw the games in return for payoffs from gamblers – beat Chicago in eight.

The "Western Avenue Orchard," as *Enquirer* sports editor Lou Smith dubbed it some years later, was a classic neighborhood park, tucked into the modest, working-class West End of Cincinnati. Parking wasn't an issue in those days; more important for the many who took a train to the game, the park was just a short walk from Union Terminal. Once the automobile gained popularity, residents on the intersecting streets near Crosley Field made side money by turning their small yards into lots that might hold six or eight cars.

Redland/Crosley was a cozy place, with a seating capacity of only 20,696 when it opened and 29,603 in its 1969, its last full season. Its trademark feature was "The Terrace" – a 15-degree incline in the grass playing surface that marked the approaching outfield walls in left, center and right. It served the purpose of today's warning track, though visiting outfielders, unfamiliar with the sudden upslope, would stumble on occasion and thus complained about it.

Perhaps Crosley Field's most significant moment in baseball history occurred May 24, 1935, when the Reds beat the Philadelphia Phillies 2-1 in the first night game played in the major leagues. At the time, team president Larry MacPhail told other club owners the Cincinnati team might have to fold because of low attendance if they didn't allow the Reds to try playing games at night. This was during the height of The Great Depression; they took MacPhail at his word.

Eight metal stanchions holding 632 lamps were erected, and President Franklin Delano Roosevelt ceremoniously pushed a button at the White House that "turned on" the lights in Cincinnati. Reds righthander Paul Derringer became the first pitcher ever to start a major league night game, facing Phillies second baseman Lou Chiozza, the first batter ever under the lights. Some 20,422 fans showed up to see it. With night baseball, Reds attendance increased by 400 percent.

Big-league baseball's first All-Star Game had been played a few years earlier, on July 6, 1933, at Comiskey Park in Chicago. It was the idea of *Chicago Tribune* sports editor Arch Ward, to coincide with the city's Century of Progress Exposition. So it was All-Star Game No. 6 that came to Crosley Field just three years after the first night game. The American League had won four of the first five, and was favored to win again. But Cincinnati's new hero, a flash for the ages, thwarted a fast start by the AL.

Three weeks before the game, Reds rookie left-hander Johnny Vander Meer had done something that hasn't been repeated since – and may never be matched – when he tossed back-to-back no-hitters. (The second came in the first night game at Ebbets Field in Brooklyn.) As the National League's starting pitcher in the 1938 All-Star Game, "Vandy" retired the first six batters he faced, including five future

Hall-of-Famers. Charlie Gehringer, Earl Averill, Jimmie Foxx, Joe DiMaggio and Bill Dickey went down on four grounders – two back to the mound – and a strikeout. Vander Meer actually came within one batter of a three-inning no-hitter, a leadoff single by Joe Cronin in the third preceding three more quick outs.

An unearned run in the first inning made Vander Meer the winning pitcher in a 4-1 victory before a crowd of 27,067 – the second-smallest attendance ever for a Major League All-Star Game. Leo Durocher, Brooklyn's mouthy shortstop, would score the National's final run – racing home all the way from first base on a throwing error by DiMaggio. Durocher would have a prominent role in the 41st All-Star Game in Cincinnati 32 years later.

The 1938 All-Star Game is remembered as Yankees great Lou Gehrig's last. After grounding out to second base as a pinch-hitter in the fifth inning, Gehrig singled in the seventh, and lined out deep to right in the ninth. He would struggle through the rest of the 1938 season, and decline rapidly the next year, collapsing during Spring Training. On May 2, after hitting only .143 in the first month of the 1939 season, he took himself out of the New York lineup, ending his consecutive-games-played streak at 2,130. He would never play again.

Gehrig delivered his famous "Luckiest Man on the Face of the Earth" speech at home plate in Yankee Stadium on July 4, 1939 – less than a year after his last All-Star at-bat at Crosley Field. He died, of the mysterious disease that has since borne his name, on June 2, 1941. He was 37.

How different was baseball, and the All-Star Game, in 1938? The time of the game was one hour and 58 minutes. And six players who eventually made it to Cooperstown – Bob Feller, Red Ruffing, Carl Hubbell, Lloyd Waner, Gabby Hartnett and Arky Vaughan – didn't get into the game.

By 1953, when the All-Star Game returned to Crosley Field, America had been through World War II and the Korean War. And Ted Williams, the greatest hitter of all time, had served in both.

Williams, who was discharged from duty as a Marine Corps pilot just four days before the 20th All-

Star Game, came to Cincinnati to throw out the ceremonial first pitch. (Richard Nixon was, by then, U.S. Vice President in Dwight Eisenhower's administration, but there's no evidence that he attended the game.) Williams subsequently would train for 10 days, then rejoin the Boston Red Sox and put up All-Star numbers, batting .407 with 13 home runs and 34 runs batted in – in 37 games.

By the early '50s, the Reds had become the Redlegs – a name change in anxious response to the so-called McCarthy Hearings (formally the House Un-American Activities Committee – HUAC), "McCarthyism" and the Communist scare they represented. Crosley Field had added a couple more distinctive aspects, as well.

The "Goat Run," a fenced area in front of the right field "Sun Deck," had been added to make it easier for "Big Klu" – sleeveless lefthanded slugger Ted Kluszewski – to hit home runs. (It worked. Big Klu hit 49 in 1954, and 47 in 1955. The Goat Run was removed in 1958, at the end of Kluszewski's playing career in Cincinnati.)

And beyond the left field wall, a sign on the Superior Towel and Linen Service plant advertised a downtown clothier, Seibler Suits, which promised a new suit to any player hitting the sign. (Rightfielder Wally Post won eleven suits to lead the Reds, and Willie Mays led all visitors with seven.) In the early 1960s the "laundry," as it was known, was demolished to create 38 precious parking spaces.

Kluszewski and centerfielder Gus Bell represented the "Redlegs" in the National League starting lineup in 1953, and the NL again won, 5-1, before a Cincinnati crowd that this time topped 30,000. The 30,802 (to be exact) saw history made when former Negro League great Satchel Paige became the oldest player ever to participate in an All-Star Game when he pitched the eighth inning for the AL at the age of 47 years, seven days. He remains the oldest All-Star ever to actually play in the game.

* * *

In its final 17 years of existence as a major league park, Crosley Field saw a thrilling but ultimately fruitless pennant race in 1956 (marked by the arrival of Rookie-of-the-Year Frank Robinson); hosted the 1961 World Series (led by NL Most Valuable Player Robinson) against the Yankees and Babe-beating home run hitter Roger Maris; witnessed the first official "save" when that statistic was established in 1969 (by Bill Singer of the Dodgers in a 3-2 Los Angeles victory on Opening Day); and enjoyed an unprecedented run of success by the home team (eight winning seasons in its last nine).

The 1956 season was something special. Collectively, those Reds slugged 221 homers to equal the National League team record set by the 1947 New York Giants – achieving the tie on a Smokey Burgess pinch-hit homer in Chicago in the next-to-last game of the season. Cincinnati still had a chance to win its first pennant since 1940 going into the last weekend – finishing third, one game out of second, two out of first.

This was the year a certain 11-year-old boy learned what SRO meant. Attendance at Crosley Field topped a million for the first time ever, totaling

1,125,928. More than once I stood in line with my dad and brother as the Standing Room Only sign went up at the ticket windows. The club attendance record stood until Riverfront Stadium, capacity 52,952, opened in 1970. Playing 45 games in the new stadium that year, the Reds' total attendance was 1,803,568.

Crosley was supposed to close at the end of the 1969 season. But completion of Riverfront Stadium was behind schedule, so the Reds began 1970 in their old home. The delayed demise finally arrived on June 24, and I feel fortunate to have covered that final game in the park's storied history. My story, for posterity and the fun of it, recorded "lasts" in the old park's 59-year history.

The Reds had the last laugh, 5-4 over the Giants, thanks to the last homer – actually, the last back-to-back homers, by Johnny Bench and Lee May, off Juan Marichal. The last win went to reliever Wayne Granger, who had set a record the previous season for most appearances in the same park. Granger replaced starter Jim McGlothlin in the eighth, and retired

Bobby Bonds – Barry's dad – for the last out, on a slow roller he fielded himself. The last pitch in Crosley Field history was a slider.

"You bet it meant something," Granger said afterwards. "It meant something to every guy on the ball club. Everyone wanted to win that last game.

"We've got 90 more games or something like that, so this should have been just another game. But I had a funny feeling inside when I came in to pitch. And it felt like we were winning the pennant or something once we got the last out. Everyone was rushing out to congratulate me and everything.

"I'll remember this for a long time. So far it's one of my biggest thrills. My biggest hasn't come yet – it will wait until October."

On this night of lasts, Pete Rose had the last triple, Bernie Carbo the last double, Tito Fuentes the last single, Hal Lanier the last walk and Bonds the last strikeout. The last Reds out was made by Darrel Chaney on a tall fly to right; the last error also belongs, forever, to Chaney. Carbo was the last player hit by a pitch, and Jimmy Stewart was the last Red to enter the last game, pinch-hitting for Carbo in the eighth.

Last but not least, Pete Rose ran the last red light at Crosley Field, ignoring third base coach Alex Grammas' stop sign to score the Reds' third run in the fifth on Bobby Tolan's single. "That wasn't a stop light; that was a caution light," Pete clarified.

A few weeks later he'd get a green light from another third base coach, and would make All-Star history.

"First Pitch" by W. F. Schildman, used with permission of CEI Sports Inc.

Riverfront

THE RACE to build a successor to Crosley Field in time for the 1970 season and the All-Star Game that summer began in early 1967 with demolition of buildings in an area between Third Street and the Ohio River known as "The Bottoms." Marked mostly by warehouses, dilapidated housing, and railroad sidings, "The Bottoms" was the birthplace of one Leonard Franklin Slye, who would become famous by another name.

Born November 5, 1911, Leonard Slye is much better known as cowboy actor and singer Roy Rogers. He appeared in more than 100 movies and countless episodes of *The Roy Rogers Show* on radio and television from the mid-30s to the 1960s. (Every Reds fan from the '40s through the '60s surely remembers his golden palomino Trigger, his German Shepherd Bullet, his singing wife Dale Evans, and their theme song, "Happy Trails.")

After Riverfront Stadium was completed, Roy Rogers joked that he had been born at second base.

A new ballpark for the Reds had been discussed as far back as 1948, but it was December 1966 before it became a reality. A group headed by Frank Dale, publisher of *The Enquirer,* acquired the ball club from William O. DeWitt, who had bought the club from the Powell Crosley estate after the successful 1961 season. The city agreed to build a new stadium when Dale's group agreed to sign a 40-year lease. At the same time, the American Football League awarded an expansion franchise to Paul Brown, who founded the Bengals and agreed to join the new Reds owners in the 40-year stadium lease.

Ground was broken on February 1, 1968, which allowed 26 months to complete construction in time for Opening Day, 1970. Estimated cost: $43 million. By April 1969, though, it was obvious the new stadium would not be finished in time for the first pitch of the 1970 season. Construction delays and other problems had thrown the project months behind schedule and added about $5 million to the price tag.

Recognizing that completion in time to allow a shakedown period – i.e. regular-season games – could not be assured, Baseball Commissioner Bowie Kuhn began making contingency plans in case the as-yet-unnamed stadium in Cincinnati was not ready for major league competition. In that event, the 1970 All-Star Game would be played in Atlanta.

Atlanta Fulton County Stadium opened in 1965, the first of several symmetrical, multi-purpose, so-called "cookie-cutter" stadiums whose design accommodated both baseball and football. Cincinnati's new stadium was the third of them, following Busch Stadium in St. Louis and preceding – by two weeks – Three Rivers Stadium in Pittsburgh, and a year later, Veterans Stadium in Philadelphia.

Cincinnati's new park would have two unique features. A track that ran through shallow left field would enable the third base stands to be moved into the outfield, thus creating a football-field configuration when the Bengals played there. And it would be the first outdoor all-artificial-turf playing surface – 120,000 square feet of synthetic grass – with a dirt sliding pit at each base and, of course, a dirt home plate area, pitching mound and warning track (no more outfield terrace). White lines painted on the turf defined what would have been the "skin" infield area, and covering the infield between games henceforth would mean spreading small tarps over the pitcher's mound, home plate area and each base cutout; since the rest of the field was synthetic turf, there was no need to protect it from rain.

Various polls and surveys advanced a variety of names for the new, round stadium. Some suggested naming it for a prominent person. Former U. S. Presidents Taft and Eisenhower, Ohio Gov. Jim Rhodes, moonwalker Neil Armstrong (who became a University of Cincinnati professor), 1961 World Series manager Fred Hutchinson, and Powell Crosley Jr., were most popular. Others favored Regal Stadium (fitting for the Queen City), Buckeye Bowl and Queen City Stadium. Five weeks before the first game was played there, Cincinnati Mayor Eugene Ruehlmann settled the issue. The project's name would be the stadium's name: Riverfront.

Anxiety mounted as "Riverfront Stadium" frantically approached completion. Would Cincinnati host the 41st All-Star Game, or would Atlanta?

A brief wire service story written June 1, 1970 provided the answer:

Baseball Commissioner Bowie Kuhn announced today that the 1970 Major League All-Star Game definitely will be played in Cincinnati July 14.

Construction disputes and other problems threatened to delay opening of the new park.

Kuhn said all facilities were expected to be in excellent shape for the All-Star Game.

The novelty of a grass-less outdoor playing field would be a topic of frequent comment in the television and radio broadcasts on July 14.

* * *

The first game in Riverfront Stadium history was played the night of June 30, exactly two weeks before the All-Star Game. Again, I was fortunate enough to be there to see it, and to write about it. This time, the theme was "firsts."

Cincinnati's inaugural opponent, as only fate could script it, was the standby host for the 1970 All-Star Game: Atlanta. The Braves exacted the only consolation they could by winning the first game ever played outdoors on wall-to-wall carpet; final score, 8-2. Felix Millan had the first hit; Hank Aaron hit the first home run; and Pat Jarvis pitched the first complete game.

Among the more obscure firsts:

Big Klu, who had returned as hitting coach, had the honor of taking the first batting practice cuts, and rapping the first BP single. Pitcher Gary Nolan, despite his .086 batting average, owns the first batting practice homer, the result of pitchers getting their licks first.

Tony Gonzalez, who broke into the majors with the Reds in 1960 but had a nice career in Philadelphia before hanging on with the Braves, chalked up the first ground-rule double when the ball he sliced over third base rolled under the movable grandstand. (It was only a matter of time before a different ground-rule double would be recorded – a fly ball that hit the turf and bounced over an outfield fence, as about two dozen balls had done during batting practice.)

Reds shortstop Woody Woodward was the first player to attempt to slide on the carpet, beginning his attempt to break up a double play before he reached the second base sliding pit in the sixth inning.

There were, of course, many firsts yet to be recorded, including the first home run by a Reds player, first balk, first Reds victory . . . and the first play at the plate.

Number14 would soon be part of that.

Tommy Helms, Klumpe/Rhodes Collection Reds Hall of Fame.

Playing To Win

IN THE 21ST century, the Major League Baseball All-Star Game is a far different event than it was in 1970. Neither the designated hitter nor interleague play – both of which fundamentally altered the All-Star Game's appeal – had yet been introduced. And cable channels ESPN and MLB Network had not yet begun to saturate homes with games from both leagues every day and night of the season.

Home Run Derby was held as part of the All-Star Game for the first time in 1985, a way to jazz up the festivities for television. Cincinnati's own Dave Parker (who starred at Courter Tech while in high school and had come to the Reds in 1984 after 11 seasons with Pittsburgh) won that first exhibition over a field of nine other stars that included Jim Rice, Carlton Fisk, Eddie Murray, Cal Ripken Jr., Dale Murphy and Steve Garvey.

And 17 years later, the 2002 All-Star Game ended in a 7-7 tie – terminated by mutual agreement of managers Joe Torre and Bob Brenly without a victor after 11 innings because they had used all 19 pitchers in an effort to get every player into the game. Promising, "This will never happen again," Commissioner Bud Selig declared that, henceforth, home field advantage in the World Series would be awarded to the league that won that year's All-Star Game. Selig wanted to ensure that the teams would play to win and that the game would reach its intended conclusion.

By contrast, in 1970 the All-Stars simply showed up the day before the game, got to know each other or renewed acquaintances in their respective locker rooms, and had a workout. The next night they went out and played to win, not because of some mandated incentive but because that's the only way they knew to play baseball. League pride was a big thing.

That attitude was tellingly evident in the comments of Reds players I interviewed for an advance story about the game – and was exhibited memorably in the game itself.

Tommy Helms, still the Reds second baseman in 1970, recalled his All-Star appearance in 1968 and, in particular, a play involving Minnesota's seven-time batting champion, Rod Carew, an 18-time All-Star and eventual first-ballot Hall-of-Famer.

"I went into second base and knocked Carew pretty good," Helms said. After the game a writer said to him, "Hey man, this is the All-Gar Game. Why go after Carew like that?"

Helms repeated his reply, word-for-word: "What if I hit him and he throws the ball in the stands instead of first base? It might mean a run for us, and that run might mean we win. That's why."

The anecdote would seem almost prophetic the next evening.

Tony Perez, the 1967 All-Star Game MVP after his 15th inning home run broke a 1-1 tie and enabled the National League to win the longest All-Star Game ever, also spoke of the importance of playing to win.

"It's important to win for the National League," he said. "This is what I feel, and what most players feel. Everyone wants to be the best.

"It will mean even more since we'll be playing in Cincinnati," he added. "It's something I feel in my body. I'm more excited. Everyone knows me and wants to see me do well. It makes me more excited, and it makes me want to do well."

* * *

As current Reds were talking up the importance of playing hard and going all out to win, one of the biggest Reds heroes of all-time, Frank Robinson, was enjoying his triumphant return as an AL All-Star for the fourth time in five seasons since his shocking trade to Baltimore before the 1966 season. He understood what Perez was saying about the Cincinnati fans.

"It was a nice place where the fans became your friends," he said of his days at Crosley Field. "If you took the runway from the clubhouse, you had to walk right through the box seats. You knew just where certain fans would be. It was almost like we were on a first-name basis with the fans.

"I've always had a fond feeling for the fans here," he added, "and I always will. The fans saw me when I first came here. They helped me through the bad times when I had to get my feet on the ground as a rookie. They stayed with me all the time. I'll feel tremendous when I take the field."

Robby, as nearly everyone called him when he played for in Cincinnati, was not yet 21 when he began his Rookie-of-the-Year season in 1956. The

"Redlegs" had integrated only two seasons earlier, with utilityman Chuck Harmon and Puerto Rican outfielder Nino Escalera. On the '56 team, Robby had three season-long black teammates: pitcher Brooks Lawrence, who won 19 in his first season after Gabe Paul acquired him in a trade from St. Louis; first baseman George Crowe, who had played with the Milwaukee Braves the previous two years; and former Negro League outfielder Bob "Swish" Thurman. Still, they were all older, veteran players – Thurman, 39, Crowe, 35, and Lawrence, 31. No one on the team, regardless of race, was as young as Robby, which made acceptance by the fans that much more important.

In that magical year when the "Redlegs" almost won the pennant, Robby tied former Boston outfielder Wally Berger's record of 38 home runs in a rookie season. He led the National League with 122 runs scored, drove in 83, and batted a solid .290. He also set the National League record – which has stood, as of 2014, for 58 years – for most times hit by a pitch for a rookie with 20.

Robby quickly earned a reputation as a fierce competitor. He slid hard in an effort to break up double plays, and often came in with spikes high. More than once, his play led to fistfights, the most notable a brawl with eventual Hall of Fame third baseman Eddie Mathews of Milwaukee in which Robby got the worst of it, though he insisted he had "won the war" even if he lost that battle.

"I won the fight," he insisted as teammates, who had seen the one-sided whipping Mathews administered, looked askance. "I had a homer and a double, drove in one run and scored another, and made a catch that robbed him of an extra base hit. And we won the second game."

Many opponents felt Robinson deliberately went out of his way to injure fielders when running the bases. "I know I felt that way before I was traded to the Reds," Don Zimmer once said. Zimmer hailed from Cincinnati's Western Hills – Pete Rose country – and was known as a tough competitor himself. "After I became Robby's teammate, I realized he was just a tremendous competitor, probably one of the most fierce I ever played with."

Robby played 10 seasons in Cincinnati, winning the National League Most Valuable Player Award in 1961, when he led the Reds into the World Series. He batted .323 that season with 37 homers and 124 runs batted in. He was traded to Baltimore after the 1965 season in the worst trade in Reds history, Bill DeWitt justifying the trade by calling him "an old 30." Those competitive juices stoked, Robby went out the next year and became the only player in baseball history to win an MVP Award in both leagues. He won the American League Triple Crown with a .316 batting average, 49 home runs and 122 RBIs.

"It would have felt a little better if we were playing back at the old park," he said at Riverfront Stadium the day before the 1970 All-Star Game. "I have a lot of memories from there. I played my first game, got my first hit and my first homer at Crosley Field. My only three-home run game in the majors came there, and both my National League grand slams.

"If we were playing there, I'd find myself saying, 'I hit a ball here,' or 'I made a catch there.' I've never played in the new park, though, so it's not quite the same."

Pete Rose's Cincinnati career overlapped Robby's for three seasons, 1963-65, and Pete's will to win was comparable, as evidenced the day before the 1970 All-Star Game.

Playing in his fifth of what would be 17 All-Star Games in a 24-year major league career, Pete cited the league pride communicated by former National League president Warren Giles, who served as general manager of the Reds from 1937 through 1951 then NL president until he retired in 1969.

"Mr. Giles sure didn't want to lose any All-Star Games," Pete said. "Anyone who ever heard him talk to the team before the game would know that. And when you hear from the big man, it makes you want to win that much more."

And then Pete said: "I play it like any other game – I play it to win."

First Fan

A CINCINNATIAN – yes, a native of the birth-place of professional baseball – began the practice of U.S. Presidents throwing out ceremonial first pitches.

Portly William Howard Taft, namesake of a main east-west connector from Columbia Parkway to Clifton and the University of Cincinnati campus, won the presidency in 1908, succeeding Theodore

Roosevelt. He would serve one term, and later become the only man ever to serve as both President and Chief Justice of the U.S. Supreme Court when another Ohioan, President Warren G. Harding, appointed him to head the high court in 1921.

A year after succeeding TR, President Taft officially commenced play between the Washington Senators and Connie Mack's Philadelphia Athletics by throwing a strike (presumably) to legendary Walter "Big Train" Johnson of the home team. It is said that it was Senators manager Jimmy McAleer's idea, though Hall of Fame righthander Johnson made the invitation. The date was April 14, 1910 – Opening Day at National Park in the capital.

Since that occasion, every U.S. President has thrown at least one ceremonial first pitch – for either a season opener, a game of the World Series, or an All-Star Game – usually in Washington. In 1970, Cincinnati's brand new Riverfront Stadium became only the fourth stadium outside the capital to host a First Fan's toss. The others: Philadelphia's Baker Bowl (Woodrow Wilson, 1915, World Series) and Shibe

Park (Herbert Hoover, 1929 and 1930, World Series both times), and Ebbets Field in Brooklyn (Dwight Eisenhower, 1955, World Series).

* * *

The Riverfront "pitch" marked the first time a President started an All-Star Game. The "hurler" was Richard M. Nixon, who had been presented with a trophy as "Baseball's Number One Fan" by Commissioner of Baseball Bowie Kuhn in 1969.

The designation seemed appropriate. Renowned *New York Daily News* sports columnist Dick Young once wrote of Richard Nixon: "This isn't a guy that shows up at season openers to take bows and have his picture taken, and has to have his Secretary of State tell him where first base is. This man knows baseball." Indeed, while Dwight Eisenhower made golf a popular presidential pastime and other presidents followed his example, Nixon attended baseball games – 11 of them while he was in office. The Baseball Writers of America went so far as to make him an honorary member. He even has his own baseball card, issued in 1972, showing him making a first pitch.

"I love the game, love the competition," he said.

At a press conference during his re-election campaign in 1972, Nixon was asked to name his favorite baseball players. That led to him compile a pair of All-Star teams, one for the period of 1925 to 1945 and the other for 1945 through 1970. Much of the work on his selections was done at Camp David, the presidential retreat where Jimmy Carter later engineered the historic Camp David Accords between Egypt and Israel.

Nixon called it, "one of the hardest assignments I have undertaken." Hank Aaron said, "He knows more about baseball than some of the people in the game . . . All I can say is that I'm quite honored."

After serving as Eisenhower's vice president for two terms, Nixon lost the 1960 presidential election to John F. Kennedy. In 1963 he moved to New York and became a senior partner in the law firm Nixon, Mudge, Rose, Guthrie & Alexander. Three years later Hall of Fame pitcher Bob Feller contacted him at the request of another eventual Hall of Famer, Robin

Roberts, who was in the final season of his 19-year career. Roberts and fellow pitcher Bob Friend wanted to recruit Nixon to run the Major League Baseball Players Association.

"He told them he would be glad to take the job," Feller recalled, "but he had political obligations so he was not in a position to do it. He offered to do the law work for them for a very reasonable amount of money." Marvin Miller became MLBPA executive director on July 1, 1966, and would change the face of major league baseball over the next 15 years. Shortly after his appointment in 1966, at Roberts' request, Miller met with Nixon before naming Dick Moss MLBPA general counsel.

In his memoir, *A Whole Different Ball Game: The Sports and Business of Baseball,* Miller wrote:

> *"I didn't want to discuss politics, and I certainly didn't want to bring up the matter of the next general counsel of the Players Association. Just before I was set to leave, Nixon's expression turned serious, or rather more serious. Here it comes, I thought. 'Mr. Miller,' he said, 'you have a very difficult job in*

front of you. Let me know if I can do anything to help you. I am on very good terms with the owners.' I thought to myself, 'Yes, I bet you are.' I expressed my thanks and headed home."

One can only imagine Miller's surprise when, almost 20 years later, the presidents of the American and National Leagues chose Nixon to arbitrate a pay dispute with the umpires over the expansion of post-season playoffs from best-of-five to best-of-seven games – and Nixon ruled in favor of the umpires!

As he listened in his Manhattan law office to the arguments both sides presented in the umpire pay dispute – sipping soda from a glass with the presidential seal – arbitrator Nixon jotted down recollections of the first major league baseball game he attended. He was then a law student at Duke University.

"I saw my first Major League Baseball game about 50 years ago," he wrote, "when I sat in the sun-drenched bleachers at Griffith Stadium on July 4, 1936 and saw the New York Yankees clobber the

Washington Senators in a doubleheader. Since then I have seen scores of games at the ballpark and on television. Sometimes I have agreed with the umpires and other times I have disagreed with them. But I have never questioned their integrity."

A "Big Stick" Adirondack baseball bat, personalized for Nixon's son-in-law, David Eisenhower, is a significant part of the story of how President Richard Nixon wound up attending the 1970 All-Star Game in Cincinnati. Adirondack produced dozens of those personalized bats as souvenirs of that game. (I have one myself.) David Eisenhower got one after suggesting to his father-in-law that he attend the 41st Midsummer Classic on July 14. The President decided to do so after making an appearance at a governor's conference 100 miles away in Louisville, Kentucky.

It should have come as no surprise that the First Fan was still in his seat to see the climactic ending.

"I never leave a game before the last pitch," he had said, "because in baseball, as in life and especially politics, you never know what will happen."

Down Under

(continued)

"ALL FACILITIES" weren't exactly in "excellent shape" at Riverfront Stadium the night of the 41st All-Star Game, as Bowie Kuhn had assured on June 1. The giant outfield scoreboard that hung above the center-field seats went blank for a time during the fourth inning. And that malfunction wasn't the only glitch.

The so-called "interview room" was a makeshift area in a large, unfinished concrete space under the seats in the lower bowl near home plate. It was defined by large tarps that hung like so much wash on a backyard clothesline. There WERE televisions mounted on tall stands, as the announcement in the Press Box promised. But the screens were BLANK. The writers, who had been assured they'd be able to see the last few innings on TV, had audio only. Technical problem, we were told. It was being worked on, we were told.

Curt Gowdy, Tony Kubek and the recently retired Mickey Mantle – just two years removed from his last All-Star Game – were in the broadcast booth for NBC. At field level was Lindsey Nelson. The telecast recorded the highest TV Nielsen Rating ever for an All-Star Game, 28.5, which equated to 16,670,000 households, a 54 share.

But for us, it might as well have been on radio only. It was as if we had stepped back in time, to 1938 in Cincinnati, when the All-Star Game could be heard but not seen.

* * *

While members of the press were making their way down under, the American League increased its lead in the top of the seventh. Facing Gaylord Perry, Brooks Robinson singled to center with one out. After Tony Oliva walked, Davey Johnson's infield single loaded the bases.

No one could have scripted the next hitter.

Ray Fosse, who had scored the AL's first run the inning before, lined out on a backhanded catch by Cito Gaston in deep center. His sacrifice fly gave the Americans a 2-0 lead.

Despite the disappointment of no picture on the TV sets under the stadium, I was excited. My assignment was the American League locker room. My mind was racing with possible angles if the AL broke its seven-game losing streak.

1970 ALL-STAR GAME · RIVERFRONT STADIUM · CINCINNATI, OHIO
OFFICIAL PROGRAM $1.00

Classic

BY 1957 the *Cincinnati Times-Star,* one of the city's two afternoon daily newspapers, was struggling financially. It would be sold to Scripps Howard, publisher of the other afternoon paper, *The Cincinnati*

Post, in July 1958, and its name added to the *Post's* nameplate for a defined length of time after the sale.

But during the 1957 baseball season, the *Times-Star* did its best to remain viable and a significant part of the community. Thus came the Great All-Star Ballot Box Stuffing Scandal. Published daily in the *Times-Star* was an All-Star ballot that encouraged fans of the "Redlegs" to get involved in selecting the 1957 National League All-Stars. It read:

'Fill Out Any Number of Ballots'
LET'S BACK THE REDLEGS!
CINCINNATI TIMES-STAR
ALL-STAR BALLOT

Below that heading was space for write-in votes, by position. "HERE ARE YOUR REDLEGS" read the heading over a box that listed Cincinnati's starters at each position. The clear suggestion was that those were the players whose names should be written on the lines alongside that box. Below a notation that pitchers would be picked by the managers appeared additional instructions that read:

Fill out any number of ballots and mail to:
All-Star, Times-Star, P.O. Box 1399,
Cincinnati 99, Ohio,
or deposit in Kroger Kwis Box at any Kroger
Supermarket, or deposit at your favorite tavern.

Next came lines for the voter's name and address, then, to wrap it up:

VOTE OFTEN – VOTE EARLY

All ballots must be received at TIMES-STAR
Before noon, Wed., June 26

COUPON WILL RUN DAILY
Baseball Commissioner Ford Frick has
designated the TIMES-STAR as the official
All-Star Game Poll newspaper in this area.

The result, predictably, was that seven Cincinnati players were elected to start the 1957 All-Star Game for the NL: second baseman Johnny Temple, short-stop Roy McMillan, third baseman Don Hoak, catcher Ed Bailey, and outfielders Frank Robinson, Gus Bell and Wally Post. Only first baseman George

Crowe, who was playing in place of injured Ted Kluszewski, was missing. A guy named Stan Musial somehow beat him out.

An investigation by Ford Frick determined that more than half of that year's All-Star ballots came from Cincinnati. Frick appointed Willie Mays and Hank Aaron to start in place of Bell, who was retained as a reserve, and Post, who was injured and unable to participate anyway. Frick also stripped fans of their right to elect the All-Star starters. Beginning in 1958, a vote of managers, players and coaches determined the entire All-Star teams for both leagues.

"I can take it if we lose, but I strongly object to one league making a burlesque of the All-Star Game," Frick said. "I never want to see such an exhibition again."

*   *   *

Fan balloting was restored, ironically, for the 1970 All-Star Game in Cincinnati. To avoid a repeat of the 1957 fiasco, 26 million ballots were evenly distributed to 75,000 retail outlets around the country, and 150 minor and major league ballparks. The Commissioner by then, Bowie Kuhn, also announced that a special panel would be in place to review voting to determine if <u>ballot stuffing</u> had occurred.

The fans, in Cincinnati and throughout baseball, could not have done better. The 1970 Major League All-Star Game was intensely competitive, ebbing and flowing with drama and genuine All-Star plays. If it had ended quietly, it still would be considered a classic for the array of all-time greats who took part.

Twenty eventual Hall of Fame players graced the All-Star rosters that year (plus the gambler who would surpass the immortal Ty Cobb in total hits and belongs in Cooperstown with them). The American League roster included the two Robinsons, Frank and Brooks; Yaz – Carl Yastrzemski; Harmon Killebrew, Luis Aparicio, Jim Palmer, Catfish Hunter and Rod Carew, who was injured and did not play. The National League team featured Bench, Perez, Aaron, Mays, Roberto Clemente, Joe Morgan, Willie McCovey, Joe Torre, and pitchers Bob Gibson, Gaylord,

Perry, Tom Seaver and Hoyt Wilhelm (who at the age of 47 years, 353 days would have broken Satchel Paige's record had he entered the game).

Two managers who made it to Cooperstown (Earl Weaver and Leo Durocher) and home plate ump Al Barlick, who would become the sixth umpire enshrined, also took part.

Interestingly, in a game that featured almost two dozen "immortals," as Hall of Famers are viewed, three one-time All-Stars would play decisive roles in the historic conclusion that was about to unfold.

* * *

Two Reds were elected starters: Perez, who had moved from first base to third to make room in the Reds lineup for Lee May, and catcher Bench. Both played six innings; neither got a hit.

Pete Rose was a reserve, chosen by manager Gil Hodges. He replaced Hank Aaron in the top of the fifth.

Trailing 2-0 as they came to bat in the bottom of the seventh, the Nationals loaded the bases with no outs against Jim Perry, Gaylord's brother. Bud Harrelson singled; Cito Gaston walked and Denis Menke was hit by a pitch. Willie McCovey came to bat, pinch-hitting for Gaylord Perry.

Were the Nationals about to turn things around?

Stretch, as he was known, grounded into a double play: Luis Aparicio, unassisted at second, to Carl Yastrzemski, who had just moved from center field to first base. A run scored on the play, but Perry then fanned Dick Allen on a called third strike to retire the side.

The great Bob Gibson entered the game as the NL's pitcher to begin the eighth, so Curt Gowdy told us. Still no picture under the stadium.

After a slow start, Gibson was on his way to a 23-win season, the most victories in any year of his illustrious 17-year career. Only two seasons earlier, as Kubek noted, he had posted an earned run average of 1.12, which greatly influenced Major League Baseball's decision to lower the pitching mound from 15 inches to 10.

But Gibson was mortal in the top of the eighth

inning. After getting Aparicio on a grounder to second, Gibby gave up singles to Yastrzemski and Willie Horton. He retired Amos Otis on a fly to Rose in right, but Brooks Robinson tripled to what we were told was deep center. Tony Oliva's fly, also to Rose in right, ended the inning.

The AL led 4-1 with six outs to go.

"Catfish" Hunter, courtesy Oakland Athletics

Comeback

NICKNAMED BY Charlie Finley as a 19-year-old because the eccentric owner of the then-Kansas City Athletics thought he should have a colorful identity, Catfish Hunter became an almost legendary pitcher during his 14-year American League career. He pitched for five World Series champions; was the first pitcher since 1915 to win 200 games by the age of 31; on May 8, 1968 pitched the first regular-season perfect game in the AL in 46 years; won the AL Cy Young Award in 1974; and that off-season set a record for a free-agent contract when he signed with the New York Yankees for five years for a "whopping" $3.35 million.

Hunter also appeared in eight All-Star Games, though with some less-auspicious results.

He was on the mound in 1967 at Anaheim Stadium – beginning a now-unimaginable fifth inning of work – when Tony Perez homered to start the 15th and win the longest All-Star Game in history (as of then) for the NL, 2-1.

And he came in to start the bottom of the ninth at Riverfront Stadium in 1970, asked to hold a 4-1 lead and close out the victory that would end the AL's losing streak. Hunter (who would develop the what by then was known as Lou Gehrig's Disease and die at the age of 53 in 1999) managed only one out, and was charged with all three of the runs the NL needed to send the game into extra innings.

Dick Dietz, a 28-year-old catcher for the Giants

making the only All-Star appearance of an otherwise undistinguished eight-year major league career, was first to face Catfish. Dietz had replaced Johnny Bench in the top of the seventh inning as the contingent of sportswriters headed below decks. Dietz would hit an even .300 in 1970 with 22 home runs and 107 runs batted in – All-Star numbers, for sure, but exactly one-third of all his major league homers, and 35.5% of all his RBIs. His lifetime batting average: .261.

In the first of his two, career All-Star plate appearances, Dietz homered over the 404-foot sign in straightaway center field to pull the NL within two at 4-2. It was only the fourth hit of the game for the NL.

Singles by Bud Harrelson and Joe Morgan (yet to be traded from Houston to Cincinnati), coming before and after a popout by San Diego's Cito Gaston – the first player ever elected to an All-Star Game solely by write-in vote in Commissioner Kuhn's closely monitored new system – put runners at first and second with one out. Willie McCovey again stepped to the plate in a clutch situation.

This time Stretch would face a lefthander – the Yankees' Fritz Peterson replaced Catfish – and this time there would be no double play. A single to center scored Harrelson to make it 4-3. Curt Gowdy noted that Morgan went from first to third.

McCovey was Peterson's only hitter. New York teammate Mel Stottlemyre, a 20-game winner three of the past four seasons, succeeded him to face Roberto Clemente, pinch-hitting for Gibson.

Hanging on the TV crew's every word, the assembled sportswriters beneath the stands heard that Clemente lined to Amos Otis in center, and that Morgan used his speed to score from third to tie the game. The winning run was on first, but Stottlemyre struck out the next hitter – Pete Rose.

"We're going to extra innings," said Gowdy.

* * *

There had been a few other dramatic ninth innings in All-Star Game history. In 1941 at Briggs Stadium in Detroit, Ted Williams capped a four-run AL rally in the bottom of the ninth with a walk-off three-run homer that produced a 7-5 victory. Johnny Callison of the Phillies matched that in 1964 at Shea Stadium in New York when his three-run walk-off completed a four-run comeback in a 7-4 NL win.

But only in 1961 did a last-ditch rally send a game into extra innings. It was July 11 at notoriously windblown Candlestick Park in San Francisco. Major League Baseball was holding two All-Star Games per season at the time, to increase the amount of money that went into the players' pension fund. (The practice, thankfully, was terminated after four seasons, 1959-62. This was Game One of the series that year.)

The NL led 3-1 when Pittsburgh's Roy Face, who had compiled a remarkable 18-1 record in relief while bringing the "forkball" into prominence in 1959, began the top of the ninth. It was the start of what would go down as two innings of the most bizarre play in All-Star history. Before that half-inning ended, the NL would make three errors; Giants reliever Stu Miller, the third pitcher in the inning, would lose his balance on the pitching rubber in a gust of wind and be called for a balk; and the AL would score twice to tie the score at 3-3.

In the top of the 10th as the blustery conditions persisted, normally reliable Cardinals third baseman Ken Boyer would make his second run-scoring error in two innings – this one a bad throw that allowed Chicago's Nellie Fox to score all the way from first base to give the AL a 4-3 lead. But in the bottom of the 10th against knuckleballer Hoyt Wilhelm, Hank Aaron led off with a single and went to second on a passed ball – the combined result of Candlestick's wind and the knuckler's flutter.

Willie Mays doubled to again tie the score; Frank Robinson was hit by a pitch that bobbed off-course in the turbulence; and Roberto Clemente singled to win it.

There were six errors, a balk, a passed ball, a hit batsman and five runs in the last two innings, and the National League won 5-4 – a score that would be repeated nine years later at Riverfront Stadium.

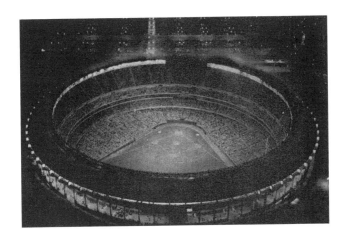

Down Under

(continued)

If only we could go back to the press box for extra innings, the marooned reporters said to each other! But this All-Star Game was so suspenseful that the President of the United States decided he'd stay and see how it would end. The elevators remained locked down.

There was no Internet in 1970. No laptops or cell phones, either. Curt Gowdy, with help from Kubek and Mantle, was our link to the outside world, or at least to the world of the game that should have been unfolding before our very eyes.

For me, this was a totally unexpected situation. I'd begun my newspaper career only five years earlier, at *The Kentucky Post* across the Ohio River in Covington. After two years there, I went to Louisville, where sportswriters wrote for both *The Courier-Journal* and *The Louisville Times*. I'd never encountered anything like this, and wondered if any of the more experienced guys in our group had.

Claude Osteen, a old-fashioned "bonus baby" from suburban Reading High who signed with the Dodgers instead of his hometown Reds (in the days before the amateur player draft), pitched the 10th, 11th and 12th for the NL, allowing a single and two doubles, but no runs. The Nationals didn't put a man on base in the extra innings until two were out in the bottom of the 12th.

"The Old Lefthander," Klumpe/Rhodes Collection Reds Hall of Fame.

Unforgettable

The most memorable moment in All-Star Game history is, for the most part, a matter of generational opinion. Or home team loyalty.

Depression-era fans might ask, for example, how anything could possibly top that moment in the very first All-Star Game when the Babe himself smacked a two-run homer to beat the National Leaguers 4-2.

Or what could be a more lasting memory, might New York Giants fans pose, than King Carl Hubbell striking out Ruth, Gehrig, Jimmie Foxx, Al Simmons and Joe Cronin – in succession! – a year later in the Polo Grounds?

For sheer drama, World War II-era American League fans can point to that three-run walk-off by Teddy Ballgame at Briggs Stadium in 1941.

And post-war National League loyalists can counter with Stan The Man's round-tripper in the 12th that capped the NL's comeback from 5-0 down in the sixth in the 6-5 victory in Milwaukee in 1955.

But only one play stands as the most replayed, most controversial – most debated – play in All-Star history. That came at Riverfront Stadium, in the bottom of the 12th inning of the 41st All-Star Game, on July 14, 1970.

Heading into that 12th inning, the National League was undefeated in extra-inning games, a perfect 5-0.

The first one came in 1950, when the Game returned to its birthplace in 1933, Comiskey Park in
Chicago. The NL had won only four of the first 16
games, but a home run by Red Schoendienst in the
14th inning won it 4-3 for the Nationals.

Five years later came Musial's blast in the 12th
off Boston's Frank Sullivan in a game played on the
day of All-Star Game founder Arch Ward's funeral.
Cincinnati's beloved Joe Nuxhall wasn't the winning
pitcher, but he made the victory possible with three-
and-a-third scoreless innings of relief.

"The Old Lefthander," as he called himself, struck
out Whitey Ford with the bases loaded to end the
eighth (yes, pitchers often hit for themselves in the All-
Star Game back then); retired Mickey Mantle and Yogi
Berra with two on to preserve the 5-5 tie in the ninth;
struck out the side in the 10th; and with two on in the
11th again retired Berra before turning the game over
to the eventual winner, Gene Conley (who also played
pro basketball for the Boston Celtics), in the 12th.

That wild, 10-inning game at windy Candlestick
Park was next, followed by a 2-1, 10-inning victory

at Busch Stadium in St. Louis in 1966, and the 15-inning marathon the next year that ended when Tony Perez took Catfish Hunter deep.

* * *

The *first* All-Star Game hit of Pete Rose's illustrious career, a single to center, began the NL's two-out rally that decided the 41st All-Star Game in the 12th inning at brand new Riverfront Stadium. In nine previous All-Star Game plate appearances, he had walked twice, laid down a sacrifice bunt and gone 0-for-6 with four strikeouts. Switching to the righthanded batter's box after striking out from the left side in his last two plate appearances on that muggy, stifling, mid-80s night in 1970, Rose had taken Ball One in the dirt, and a high pitch for Ball Two. It was the only hit by a Reds player that night – between them, Bench, Perez and Rose had struck out seven times.

An established star but not yet the bigger-than-life figure he would become, the player many called Charlie Hustle was on his way to his fifth 200-hit season in eight years in the majors, and was a third of the way to his record-setting 4,256 career hits that surpassed Ty Cobb. He had won back-to-back National League batting titles in 1968 and 1969 to go with his 1963 Rookie of the Year Award, and he had realized his stated goal of becoming "the first $100,000 singles hitter" with his 1970 contract. But his Most Valuable Player Award was still three seasons away.

The American League pitcher in the 12th inning was Clyde Wright, a California Angels lefthander who won 100 and lost 111 in a 10-year career. Wright, whose son Jaret pitched for Cleveland in the 1997 World Series, had been released on waivers by the Angels at the end of the 1969 season. But at the urging of teammate Jim Fregosi, he played winter ball where he experimented with a screwball and change-up that revived his career. Resigned by California the next spring, Wright would have a career year in 1970. He went 22-12 with a 2.83 ERA; pitched a no-hitter on July 3, 1970; and was named AL Comeback Player of the Year. His All-Star Game appearance came just 11 days after he no-hit the Oakland A's.

With Rose on first, Wright faced Billy Grabarke-witz, a 24-year-old Dodgers infielder in his first full major league season. Grabarkewitz would be out of the majors by 1975, but in the year of his only All-Star Game, he would hit a solid .289 with 17 homers and 84 RBI – more than half his career totals of 28 home runs and 141 runs batted in. He was fourth in the league with a .341 average at that point in the season.

Grabarkewitz, who had replaced the Reds' Tony Perez in the top of the seventh, fell behind 0-2, then worked the count back to even before he singled just under the glove of shortstop Luis Aparicio. Willie Horton, who had replaced Frank Robinson in left field in the bottom of the sixth, fielded the ball and held Rose to second base.

In his field level seat, President Nixon looked on expectantly. Watching from the American League dugout, Frank Robinson knew it was a pivotal moment in the game. Down under, the writers waited anxiously to hear what happened next. For Clyde Wright it was, effectively, sudden death on every pitch.

The batter was Chicago's Jim Hickman, who had made it to the majors as a member of the woeful Mets in their expansion year, 1962, and hadn't had a batting average above .257 before 1970. That year, his third with the Cubs, he would hit .315 with 32 home runs and 115 runs batted in — numbers he would never approach again en route to a .252 life-time average.

Nationals manager Gil Hodges had named Hick-man to the NL All-Star team, choosing him over Cubs teammate Billy Williams. Hickman was batting .335 with 19 homers and 63 runs batted in, but the choice over Cubs hero Williams, who also was having a big season, was nonetheless controversial, at least in Chicago. In his only All-Star Game appearance, Hick-man would go 1-for-4 but become part of history.

The first two defensive substitutions in the game, entering in the top of the fifth, Rose and Hickman wound up playing one inning short of a regulation game. With two out in the bottom of the 12th, Rose moved away from second base with the potential winning run. Hickman took the first two pitches, a ball then a strike at the knees. He rifled Wright's third pitch to center field, and Amos Otis of the Kansas City Royals charged forward to field it and throw home.

Otis had started with the Mets, too, appearing in 19 games as a 20-year-old in 1967 and 48 more two years later. That was 1969, when Major League Baseball added four expansion teams: Montreal, San Diego, Seattle and Kansas City. He was traded to the Royals at the end of their inaugural season, on December 3, 1969, for third baseman Joe Foy.

Foy lasted only one year with the Mets, while Otis became the new franchise's first mainstay, appearing in five All-Star Games during 14 seasons in Kansas City and playing in the 1980 World Series, in which he batted .478 with three home runs and seven runs batted in. In 1970 he became the first Royals player to *play* in an All-Star Game. (Catcher Ellie Rodriguez represented KC the year before, but didn't get into the game.)

Otis, who had ended the top of the 12th with a flyout to Roberto Clemente with runners on first and second, came up throwing. Rose was racing around third, urged on by Leo Durocher, who had circled the bases on his own frantic All-Star sprint at Crosley Field more than 30 years before. Durocher was racing homeward, windmilling his arm as third base coaches do when waving a runner to the plate.

Durocher was yelling, "You gotta go! You gotta go!"

Ernie Lombardi, Klumpe/Rhodes Collection Reds Hall of Fame

Play At The Plate

HOME PLATE collisions were rare in baseball through the 1960s, but one of the most famous occurred – naturally – in Cincinnati in 1939. The Reds were back in the World Series for the first time since 1919, battling the seemingly invincible New York Yankees. The score was tied 4-4 in the top of the 10th inning of Game Four at Crosley Field. The Yanks held a commanding 3-0 Series lead.

With physically imposing rookie Charlie Keller on first and scrappy Frank Crosetti on third, Joe DiMaggio lined a single to left. Crosetti scored easily, and when Reds left fielder Ival Goodman bobbled the ball, Keller kept going as he rounded third. Keller and Goodman's throw arrived at virtually the same instant, and Keller – nicknamed "King Kong" because of his strength – flattened Reds catcher Ernie Lombardi, who was no small man himself at 6 feet 3 and an estimated 250 pounds.

An eight-time All-Star, 1938 National League Most Valuable Player, one of only two catchers in baseball history to win a batting title, and eventually a Cooperstown inductee, Lombardi was known fondly as "The Schnoz" for his large nose. The impact with Keller left Lombardi lying in the dust of home plate, too dazed to retrieve the ball, which was nearby. DiMaggio circled the bases to score the third run of that play, and the Yankees won 7-4 to complete the four-game sweep for their fourth straight Series victory.

The play became known as "The Schnoz's Snooze."

Seventy-two years later another burly outfielder, though one of considerably less acclaim, was involved in what has been ranked behind "The Schnoz's Snooze" as the third worst home plate collision in baseball history. On May 25, 2011, in the 12th inning of a 6-6 tie at AT&T Park in San Francisco, Miami Marlins outfielder Scott Cousins tagged up to attempt to score on a fly ball to right-center field. Cousins crashed into Giants catcher Buster Posey, and Posey suffered season-ending injuries – a fractured fibula and torn ligaments in his ankle.

Cousins said he hit Posey intentionally in order to score. "If you hit them, you punish them and you punish yourself, but you have a chance of that ball coming out." He also said, "I certainly didn't want him to get hurt." Cousins received death threats, and the play ultimately led to a rule change in 2014 concerning plays at the plate.

The key provisions of Rule 7.13 are:

- A runner may not run out of a direct line to the plate in order to initiate contact with the catcher, or any player, covering the plate. If he does, the umpire can call him out even if the player taking the throw loses possession of the ball.

- The catcher may not block the pathway of a runner attempting to score unless he has possession of the ball (or, later clarified, the ball arrives ahead of the runner). If the catcher blocks the runner before he has the ball, the umpire may call the runner safe (unless, as clarified, the ball arrives before the runner).

Predictably, Pete Rose was asked to comment on the rule change, and, as expected, he objected to it.

"What are they going to do next, you can't break up a double play?" Rose told the Associated Press. "You're not allowed to pitch inside. The hitters wear more armor than the Humvees in Afghanistan. Now you're not allowed to try to be safe at home plate? What's the game coming to? Evidently, the guys making all these rules never played the game of baseball."

*   *   *

What transpired on the night of July 14, 1970 as Pete Rose arrived at home plate will forever be as much a part of baseball lore as "The Schnoz's Snooze." Rose wiped out Ray Fosse, who had replaced starter Bill Freehan of the Tigers in the bottom of the fifth, and the National League won for the eighth straight year, 5-4.

"That's why Pete Rose earns $100,000 a year for playing baseball," wrote David Condon in the *Chicago Tribune*. "It was the type of block that would have a Kansas City Chiefs tackle blush."

"Sure, Pete Rose could have slid around Ray Fosse," *New York Daily News* columnist Dick Young wrote in *The Sporting News*. "And (Hall of Fame running back Jim) Brown could have tried to out-nifty more guys instead of running over them . . . Pete Rose has long been commended for his way. He has been tagged Charley Hustle, and he wears it proudly."

On the NBC broadcast, Curt Gowdy observed Rose checking on the injured Fosse after the play. "Now look at Rose helping Fosse up," he told the national TV audience. "No hard feelings. Baseball is that kind of game."

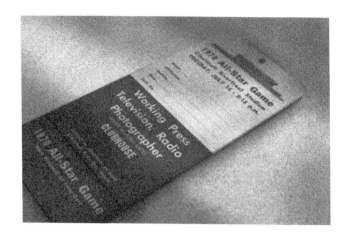

Locker Room

AS SOON as I heard Curt Gowdy say Rose had scored the winning run by crashing into Ray Fosse, I headed for the American League locker room. To this day I have no idea what Gowdy, Kubek and Mantle had to say about the play at the plate in their post-game comments, nor how many times it was replayed on the TV broadcast that we couldn't see in the bowels of Riverfront Stadium.

I couldn't imagine Fosse's condition; didn't even know if he was hurt, though it sounded as if he might be banged up in some way. (On the radio broadcast, which I heard years later, Hall of Famer Sandy Koufax, who was making a short-lived attempt at doing color commentary, said, "The only thing I can hope is that Ray Fosse wasn't hurt. You hate to see anybody hurt in the All-Star Game.")

The game lasted three hours and 19 minutes – the length of many nine-inning games 40 years later but unusually long in 1970, extra innings notwithstanding. The game had begun at 8:15 p.m. – much later than any game does in the 21st century – so my deadline was fast approaching. I had to work quickly in a locker room that was bound to be an unhappy place, to say the least. And then I'd have to find a phone and dictate my story to someone back in the sports department who would type it as I spoke it. (We were still using manual typewriters then, and stories still had to be typeset by printers working at Linotype machines.)

In my first five years of what would be a 42-year newspaper career, including three at *The Louisville Times & Courier-Journal,* I'd had plenty of unique experiences. I covered the only Kentucky Derby in which the winner (Dancer's Image) failed the post-race drug test and was disqualified; had been invited to accompany legendary basketball coach John Wooden to his hotel room during the 1967 NCAA Men's Division1 Basketball Finals – by the man himself – so we could have a private chat for a story about him and his star at the time, a guy then named Lew Alcindor; reported on equally legendary Paul Brown's 300th coaching victory; and had interviewed heavyweight boxing champion Joe Frazier in the back of a taxi as he hustled to catch a flight to New York.

But none of those moments prepared me for the bizarre events of the 1970 All-Star Game.

The obvious angle was the play at the plate, but I didn't know if Fosse would be able, much less willing, to talk about it. With time running out for me, I had to come up with an idea, something that would do justice to the memorable game I had just heard but not seen. As a young guy who hadn't been on the staff at *The Enquirer* for a year yet, I was feeling, if not panic, considerable anxiety. The last thing I wanted to do was come up empty, or file a weak story.

And then I spotted Frank Robinson, still in uniform even though he had left the game about two hours earlier. Asking the Cincinnati icon to comment on what sounded like a controversial play by a former Reds teammate seemed a natural, and something I should be able to get quickly. I figured Robby would be willing to talk with me since I'd interviewed him the day before.

I approached him as he sat on a bench in front of his locker. I introduced myself and reminded him that we had chatted the day before. He was untying the laces on his spikes, looking down. If he remembered me, it wasn't obvious. He grunted or mumbled; hardly a welcoming response.

Having spent six innings under the stadium, I had to be vague. I began with a throwaway line to get the conversation started, something like, "Tough way to lose a ball game, huh?"

Robby kept looking down, worked on his cleats and grunted.

A standard technique when interviewing a subject who is not responsive is to find different ways to ask essentially the same question, in hopes that a variation in phrasing eventually elicits a useable quote. When television reporters employ this approach, they often sound silly because it's obvious that they're saying practically the same thing repeatedly. But it works for print reporters because readers only see the eventual answer.

So I tried asking Robby about the deciding play a few different ways. Always, though, all I got were more grunts and useless one-word replies; nothing on which I could base a story. Clearly, he was in no mood to talk about the bitter ending.

Finally, somewhat in desperation, I asked point-blank: "Frank, do you think it was a dirty play?"

At this, Robinson looked up at me, while still seated and bending over his feet.

"You saw the play," he said. "What do you think?"

Frank Robinson en route to Rookie-of-the-Year,
Klumpe/Rhodes Collection Reds Hall of Fame.

'Robby Raps Pete'

I COULDN'T very well say, "Actually, Frank, I didn't see the play. I've been under the stadium for the last six innings."

So I said, "Frank, nobody cares what I think. They want to know what you think."

Robby's only response was to get up and begin circulating through the clubhouse, stopping to talk with a few players. I got my story – headlined 'Robby Raps Pete" – by shadowing him and listening carefully to everything that was said.

First stop was Fosse, who'd reached base twice on a single and a walk, scored one run and driven in another, and caught eight sweaty innings.

"Could he have gotten around you?" Robby asked. A large ice pack applied to his bruised shoulder, Fosse replied: "Yeah. He could have slid and gotten his hand in."

Waiting to be taken to Christ Hospital for X-rays, Fosse added: "I thought we were going to get him. Then he hit me."

Robinson stopped to talk briefly with Frank Howard, the towering outfielder who had hit 24 home runs for the Washington Senators so far that season. "He didn't have to do that to Fosse," Robby said. The 6-foot-7, 260-pound Howard nodded.

Robby's manager, Earl Weaver, lamented the apparent injury to Fosse, but defended Rose's decision to ram the AL catcher. "That's definitely the only way to play," he said. "You play to win. You don't compromise."

Across the dressing room from Weaver, Boston's Carl Yastrzemski, named the game's most valuable player despite playing for the losing side, was answering questions. Yaz had tied two All-Star Game records with three singles and four hits, while playing the entire 12 innings. He drove in the AL's first run, scored its third in the eighth, and played outstanding defense both in center field and at first base. His double in the top of the 12th had given the AL a chance to take the lead before the fateful bottom of the inning.

Minnesota's Harmon Killebrew, the American League home run leader with 26 and the 1969 AL Most Valuable Player, stopped to shake his hand. "Nice hitting, Carl," he said. "I thought we had them."

Yastrzemski shook his head. "Boy, this stuff (losing to the NL) is unbelievable. In the ninth inning I thought it was all over. Then . . .

"Boy, am I tired," he added. "I didn't expect to play the whole game. It took a lot out of me."

My story was coming together, but I still didn't have a direct quote from Frank Robinson regarding the decisive play. So I tried another approach, asking him how he would have handled the moment had he been trying to score the winning run.

"Slide, man," he answered emphatically. "That's the only way I would have gone in. Slide."

Delayed Replay

SINCE I HADN'T seen the play, I couldn't agree or disagree with Frank Robinson. And decades passed, believe it or not, before I watched the videotape – yes, back then it was still videotape. But after viewing the play years later, I would point out that Fosse was at least three feet, maybe four, up the third base line, in the path to home plate, awaiting the throw from Amos Otis.

Fosse was so far up the line, in fact, that the NL's on-deck batter, Dick Dietz, was behind him – also in front of home plate – signaling for Rose to slide. Still wearing his shin guards, Dietz moved out of the way before Rose barreled into Fosse, and tended to the fallen players in the dusty aftermath.

Had Rose attempted a slide, he almost certainly would never have reached the plate. He would have been tagged out, and, if it had been his usual head-first dive, could have suffered a serious injury if his head had struck Fosse's shin guards.

And as Pete had told me the day before, "I play it to win."

On the video Rose appears, almost imperceptibly, to commence his trademark lunge, but pulls up when he realizes he'll never reach the plate if he goes into a head-first slide. It all happens in a split second: Rose puts a shoulder into Fosse as the ball arrives; Fosse is separated from his glove as he literally does a full somersault; Rose is safe at home. The NL wins 5-4.

Those nine seconds of action have been digitized and rerun thousands of times on television and on-line. The play has been criticized, defended and otherwise debated for decades, and Rose and Fosse have commented over and over on that moment and its aftermath. They will be asked about it for as long as they live.

The headline on an interview before the 2013 All-Star Game reads: **"Fosse still aching, but not bitter 43 years after All-Star Game."**

The headline on a story before the 2014 All-Star Game reads: **"Fosse still bitter about Pete Rose collision in 1970 All-Star Game."**

The latter, contradictory characterization, seems based on Fosse's disagreement with Rose's oft-repeated account that the two had been to dinner, along with Sam McDowell and their wives, the night before, and that they went back to Rose's home and hung out until the wee hours.

In the 2013 interview, with CBSSports.com, Fosse confirmed a couple of key points about the fateful play – his positioning and Rose's intent – and spoke positively about his baseball career.

"As a catcher, I positioned myself where the ball

was being thrown by Amos Otis," he said. "I was up the line, not trying to block anybody. I was taught as a catcher, catch the ball and try to plant the tag. You watch the replay, which I've seen a million times. He starts to go into a head-first slide, and he sees me."

So common in sports today, the MRI (magnetic resonance imaging test) had not been invented yet in 1970. X-rays the night of the all-Star Game were negative. Fosse simply rested, then resumed playing when the pain in his left shoulder subsided to a simple throb. He finished 1970 with a .307 batting average, 18 home runs and 61 runs batted in. A year later the shoulder still ached, and another set of X-rays revealed a fracture and a shoulder separation that by then had healed, though improperly, in place.

Fosse won the Gold Glove as best defensive catcher in 1970 and was a Gold Glover and an All-Star again the next season. But his batting average in 1971 was .276 – 31 points below his 1970 average, and his home run total dropped to 12. He went from the most promising young catcher in the American League to a journeyman during his remaining eight seasons.

If he could change the outcome of that play at the plate in 1970, Ray Fosse certainly would. But he can't, and says he has no regrets about his career in baseball. "It's been good," Fosse told CBSSports.com. "I wouldn't change it for the world."

Jim Delaney interviewing Richard Nixon, courtesy Jim Delaney

Airport Stakeout

BY STAYING to see how the extra-inning All-Star Game ended, President Nixon not only kept dozens of sports writers in limbo in the depths of Riverfront Stadium, but he also left Secret Service agents and a few journalists, including a local television reporter and his cameraman, cooling their heels for more than two hours at Greater Cincinnati Airport.

Jim Delaney, then of Channel 9, hot-footed it out to CVG after using his Cincinnati Police Department contacts to nab an interview with the voluptuous stripper Morgana Roberts at the District One Station. Known as The Kissing Bandit, Morgana was famous for her forays onto playing fields to smooch players, particularly Reds stars, between innings. Yaz was batting in the top of the first, awaiting Tom Seaver's second pitch, when Morgana made her break for the All-Star playing field. She never actually made it across the foul lines this time, as she was intercepted and hauled off by Cincinnati's Finest.

Delaney and his partner dropped off the recorded interview with Morgana in time for the film – yes, film – to be processed and aired on the 11 o'clock news. Then they headed across the river into Kentucky, where the Greater Cincinnati Airport is located.

Figuring the leader of the free world would soon excuse himself to hop Air Force One back to Washington, Delaney and a few others, including a wire service reporter, set up a stakeout of sorts at the General Aviation Terminal at what was then a much more modest airport than today's sprawling installation. They waited behind a rope line about 20 yards from the tarmac where the President's limousine was expected to pull up at any minute.

Neither these reporters, nor the Secret Service, understood Richard Nixon's love for baseball.

As they waited, the reporters and Secret Service agents chatted. (Heightened security was still decades away.) Eventually word came that the National League had tied the game in the bottom of the ninth, and that the President wasn't going anywhere until he new the outcome. Later, Delaney was informed by someone at the TV station that the National League had won, and that Pete Rose had scored the winning run. There was no mention of the play at the plate.

This was five years before TV stations began using "live remote" technology. Cameramen carried heavy 16 mm cameras and light packs powered by batteries – mounted on their shoulders. Delaney conspired with cameraman Dave Arnold, planning just how they'd get an interview with the President as he exited the limo, before he moved to Air Force One.

They had to get Nixon's attention, Delaney said. He instructed Arnold to turn on his filming light the instant Nixon began to climb out of the car.

It was after midnight by the time the presidential motorcade pulled up. The light went on just as Nixon began to emerge from the back seat of his ride. It got his attention, as expected, and Delaney started toward him. He felt the hand of a Secret Service agent grab his waistband and belt from behind. But the agent didn't restrain him; he simply followed, ready to tug him away at the first false move.

"Mr. President!" Delaney called. "What did you think of the game?"

"What an exciting game," the First Fan responded. "It was especially exciting the way the local boy made the play of the game."

Delaney tried to follow up with a serious "news" question about his meetings in Louisville and Cincinnati, but the President gave him only a standard response about how nice it was "to be with the people." The entire filmed exchange lasted one minute and two seconds.

Richard Nixon won re-election to a second term in 1972, but within two years was forced to resign in the wake of the Watergate burglary scandal – the only American president ever to relinquish the office voluntarily before completing his term. His reputation as a baseball expert never diminished, though, as evidenced in 1985 when he was chosen to arbitrate that pay dispute between Major League Baseball and the Major League Umpires Association. (More than the mere ruling in favor of the umpires, Nixon's award of a 40% increase in postseason pay shocked many in the baseball world.)

The Richard M. Nixon Presidential Library and Museum in Yorba Linda, California includes appropriate recognition of his lasting status as First Fan. Among the artifacts in the exhibit titled "Play Ball! Presidents and Baseball" which opened in 2014 is correspondence between President Nixon and baseball greats such as Jackie Robinson, Nolan Ryan, Daryl Strawberry and others. Also in the collection is David Eisenhower's "Big Stick" Adirondack souvenir bat from the 1970 All-Star Game.

Bernie Carbo at Spring Training in 1970, Cincinnati Reds Hall of Fame

Deja vu

FRANK ROBINSON returned to Cincinnati later in 1970, to lead Baltimore against Pete Rose and the Reds in the World Series. The Orioles won the

American League East Division with 108 victories, and swept the Minnesota Twins, West Division winners, to claim the AL pennant. The Reds set a club record with 102 victories in winning the National League West, then swept Pittsburgh's East Division winners, to win the NL championship.

Robby hit two home runs and drove in four runs, and had six hits in 22 at-bats, a .273 average. Rose went 5-for-20, a .250 average, hit one homer, and drove in two. Baltimore won in five games.

Ironically, the Series had its own controversial play at the plate, though not involving Pete Rose. This time, I saw it unfold.

Bernardo Carbo was the Reds' first-round draft pick in the 1965 amateur draft. He was not yet 18 years old. Before his twenty-third birthday he was a full-time major leaguer, finishing second to Montreal pitcher Carl Morton in Rookie-of-the-Year voting in 1970 after batting .310 with 21 homers and 63 runs batted in. Two years later the Reds would trade him to St. Louis, the beginning of a major league odyssey that saw Bernie Carbo play for five teams in the next nine seasons.

But in 1970, he was a key figure in Game One between the Reds and Orioles.

In the sixth inning, with the score tied 3-3, Cincinnati had Carbo on third and Tommy Helms on first. Ty Cline, pinch-hitting for shortstop Woody Woodward, hit a high chopper right in front of home plate. Umpire Ken Burkhardt darted from behind the plate to make the "fair" or "foul" call as Carbo sprinted in from third on Burkhardt's blind side.

Orioles catcher Elrod Hendricks attempted a diving tag, and Burkhardt, as he was tumbling backward and unable to clearly see if the tag was made, incorrectly called Carbo out. Baltimore would score once in the next inning, and win the pivotal opener 4-3.

The same Reds players I quoted before that summer's All-Star Game weighed in critically.

"There's no way he could make that call," said Helms. "He didn't even see the play," mumbled a disbelieving Tony Perez. "He can't call him out if he doesn't see the play, and he couldn't have seen it."

Rose, of course, was asked for his opinion.

"It was a tough call," he said. "He made a bad

call, but he didn't do it deliberately." Then, as if reflecting back to the All-Star Game at Riverfront a few months earlier, Rose said in reference to Carbo: "He could have slid in and taken both of them (the catcher and the umpire) out of the play."

Ray Fosse, courtesy Oakland Athletics

Denouement

RAY FOSSE was voted the AL's starting catcher in the next year's All-Star Game, but did not play because of a torn ligament in his left hand, suffered while swinging at a Denny McLain pitch a few games before the All-Star break. It would be his only other All-Star Game selection.

Frank Robinson was chosen All-Star Game Most Valuable Player in 1971, when the American League ended its losing streak, 6-4, at Tiger Stadium in Detroit. It was Robby's two-run homer in the bottom of the third off Pittsburgh's Dock Ellis that put the AL ahead for good at 4-3. Pete Rose entered the game on defense in the bottom of the eighth inning, and didn't bat in the ninth.

In 1975 Robby became the first black manager in the major leagues when he assumed the helm of the Cleveland Indians. A player-manager that year, Robby homered in his first at-bat, one of nine in only 118 official at-bats. In 1981, he would become the first black manager in the National League, too, with the San Francisco Giants. In all, he managed five teams over 16 seasons between 1975 and 2006; was voted AL Manager of the Year in 1989 with the Orioles; and in April 2006 became the 53rd manager in history to win at least 1,000 games. He also has held positions in Major League Baseball, including, for a time, chief disciplinarian.

Fosse was traded to Oakland in 1973, and played on back-to-back World Series champions – an experience that eluded many great players. (Mr. Cub, the great Ernie Banks, for example, never made it to the post-season.)

Fosse returned to the Indians in 1976 and played for his former All-Star Game teammate for two seasons. In 1976 Fosse batted .301 with two homers and 30 runs batted in for Robinson as Cleveland finished with an 81-78 record. Fosse ended his career in 1979 with a lifetime batting average of .256 with 61 home runs and 324 runs batted in for 924 games over 12 seasons. He then became an Oakland A's broadcaster, calling their games for more than 30 years.

Riverfront Stadium hosted another All-Star Game in 1988, this one a 2-1 American League victory devoid of controversy. (By then, Pete Rose had retired.) The ballpark was renamed Cinergy Field in September 1996, around the same time voters approved construction of its replacement, Great American Ball Park, which opened in 2003. By 2015 when the Game returned to Cincinnati, more All-Star

Games had been played since the historic 1970 game than had been contested before it.

Pete Rose left the Reds after the 1978 season for Philadelphia, but returned in 1984. Upon his arrival, he followed Frank Robinson's career path – becoming a player-manager. Being a player-manager sparked his waning offense, as it had done Robby's. In the 26 games he played after returning to the Reds in 1984, he batted .365.

Rose broke Ty Cobb's record for career hits the following season – on 9/11, a date that had no other significance then – and ended his career with 4,256 (in 3,562 regular-season games). Of that amazing total number of hits, 3,358 came as a member of the Reds. (Rose also had 86 hits in postseason, to go with seven in 33 official All-Star at-bats.)

After 1970, Rose would play in 12 more All-Star Games – making 17 in all, at a record five positions (second base, left field, right field, third base and first base).

He scored only two other All-Star Game runs.

Author's Note

MY SPORTSWRITING career came to an end in December 1975. I was named an assistant city editor at *The Enquirer* at the start of 1976, and about six months later advanced to city editor – the toughest newspaper job I ever had. I directed coverage of the Beverly Hills Supper Club fire, which killed 165 on Memorial Day weekend of 1977. Our work was nominated for a Pulitzer Prize, though we didn't win it.

In 1982 I moved to the *Rocky Mountain News* in Denver – as executive sports editor. My return to sports was short-lived, though. I went into the newsroom two years later, and in 1991 the publisher asked me to try my hand at labor relations, which is the second hardest job I've ever had. The Rocky had eight unions.

I never lost my love for sports, and baseball in particular.

Acknowledgments

WHILE CITY Editor at *The Cincinnati Enquirer,* I supervised a group of young, talented reporters that included a guy named John Erardi. We called him "E" or "Big E," in part because he was a big, strapping young man. He was a "go-to" guy then, and even more so in this project. "E" eventually left local news for sports, and wound up covering the Reds. Though years went by without us ever communicating in any way, we remained friends. And when John learned about my idea for this book, he jumped all-in. An author himself, John has written books about Pete Rose breaking Ty Cobb's hit record, and about the wire-to-wire National League champion Reds of 1990 (who also won the World Series), among several. For me he opened doors in numerous ways. A mere "thank you" is not enough.

Another former *Enquirer* colleague, and a friend

I have kept up with through the years, is Jim Delaney, who founded Sentimental Productions after leaving the newspaper business. His part of the 1970 All-Star Game story is told in the chapter titled "Airport Stakeout." He shared that with me for the first time in the summer of 2014, while we were catching up over a casual dinner outside in Northern Kentucky during a visit that summer. He graciously replayed it for me when I called early in 2015. Over the years, Jim has been a source of both advice and encouragement through several book projects. My appreciation exceeds words in his case, too.

And at the risk of overwhelming readers with old *Enquirer* ties, I would be derelict if I did not thank my first boss at the paper, Jim Schottelkotte, for his faith in me, first in hiring me and then assigning me to that All-Star Game. Every career needs a few people who move it forward in various ways. Jim is one of them in my case.

If there is a more talented designer than Scott Johnson, I haven't met him or her. And Scott is a baseball nut extraordinaire, to boot. He not only dressed up this work with his unique creativity, but also enhanced the content with a baseball-fan's careful reading of the manuscript. Scott even contributed to the research that enriched the detail in the re-creation of the play-by-play.

Jon Rizzi is to editing what Scott Johnson is to design. His attention to detail and knowledge of seemingly obscure baseball facts is jaw-dropping, and the "writer's sense" and care evident in his work is the best a writer can hope for. Whoever said, "The best editor is invisible," had Jon in mind.

The starting time of this game is something I'd long forgotten, yet it was important to the telling of the story because the game ran so long, and because of the way events unfolded. Pamela Hallaren, a re-search librarian in the Arapahoe Library District in Arapahoe County, Colorado, tracked that down for me. And it was no easy task. She also pursued other valuable historic details and references. Pamela is part of the ALD's "Ask A Librarian" program, a tremen-dous resource for the citizens of the library district, whether they're writing a book, looking for a new job, or just curious about something. Thank you, Pamela.

I'd never met Chuck Pyle before I discovered his tremendous illustration of the Rose-Fosse collision. I still haven't met him in person. But I am indebted to him for his willingness to allow the use of that work of art on the cover of this book. It is an honor to be able to have such talent associated with my writing.

Finally, no one has supported and encouraged my writing the way my dear wife Melanie has and does. We are closing in on 50 years, and I can't imagine accomplishing this or anything else I've undertaken in my life without her cheering me on.

About the Author

Denny Dressman is a 2008 inductee into the Denver Press Club Hall of Fame; a past president of the Colorado Press Association; and a previous winner of the Ohio Associated Press Sports Editors' Award for Best Sports Column as well as recipient of numerous other writing awards. He currently is vice president of the Colorado Authors' League, responsible for enrichment programs; writes regularly for

Colorado Avid Golfer magazine; and teaches writing classes in the University of Denver University College adult enrichment program.

A career newspaperman, he worked for *The Kentucky Post; The Louisville Times & Courier-Journal; The Cincinnati Enquirer,* from 1969 to 1982; the *Oakland Tribune,* where he was editor; and the *Rocky Mountain News* during a 43-year career. He retired in 2007 after 25 years at the *News,* including 10 outside the newsroom as vice president for labor and human resources.

HEARD but not SEEN is his seventh book. He also has edited four others. A native of Northern Kentucky, he lives in Denver, Colorado with his wife Melanie.

DISCARD

21497050R00075